God's pron and his gracious law

Walter C. Kaiser

THE CHRISTIAN INSTITUTE

CHRISTIAN INFLUENCE IN A SECULAR WORLD

This booklet is reprinted from an article which first appeared in
Journal of the Evangelical Theology Society (JETS 33/3, September 1990, 289-302).
Used by kind permission.

First printed in October 2005

ISBN 1 901086 32 1

Published by The Christian Institute
PO Box 1, Newcastle upon Tyne, NE7 7EF

The Christian Institute is a Company Limited by Guarantee, registered in England as a charity.
Company No. 263 4440, Charity No. 100 4774.

Contents

God's promise plan and his gracious law

Foreword

The way to test the greatness and incisiveness of any truly evangelical theology is to ask how it relates Biblical law to God's gospel of grace. The history of the Church's achievement on this issue has not been remarkable or convincing.

The so-called three uses of the law were vigorously debated by the Reformers, and more recently by their descendants, but with few clear exegetical results that have stood the test of time. It is no wonder, then, that when "dominion theology," under the leadership of Greg L. Bahnsen,[1] raised the question of law and grace in a form that few had ever thought of before, a cry of "legalism" went up from evangelicals and fundamentalists. Not only were the traditional unanswered questions of law versus grace and continuity versus discontinuity between the Testaments brought to the forefront again, but now there was added the unresolved issue of the political use of the law. The law/grace question must now be answered in the larger context of the Church/state tension. Was Martin Luther's model of the two kingdoms correct? Suddenly we were no longer dealing merely with matters of soteriology and the problem of relating the Abrahamic-Davidic-new covenant to the Mosaic covenant. Now we had to settle all those questions in the context of a fairly extensive ecclesiology and eschatology. Bahnsen, Rousas John Rushdoony, Gary North, David Chilton and James B. Jordan[2] have unleashed a number of furies from a theological Pandora's box. Life will never be the same. But this is not all bad, for the Church has always found that challenges have forced her to grow in her doctrinal expression.

In order to clear the ground, as it were, a number of firmly-held interpretive principles must be faced. Each of them exercises so strong an influence over the discussion of law and gospel that no exegetical progress can be made on our understanding of the uses of the law in the life of the Christian community until we come to some agreement on this part of evangelical traditional theology.

Is the law an indivisible unity?

Most fundamental to all of these principles is this: The law is an indivisible unity.[3] Any attempt to divide the law, it is strenuously argued, is wrongheaded and will result in almost certain error. Accordingly if the law has been set aside in any sense, then it naturally follows that the whole law has been abrogated and the Christian has nothing more to do with it.

Arguments for this all-or-nothing case include three texts: (1) "For whoever keeps the whole law and yet stumbles at just one point is guilty of breaking all of it" (Jas 2:10); (2) "Again I declare to every man who lets himself be circumcised that he is obligated to obey the whole law" (Gal 5:3); (3) "Anyone who breaks one of the least of these commandments and teaches others to do the same will be called least in the kingdom of heaven" (Matt 5:19). The point that is usually made for all three of these passages is that "all" (*pantōn*) means every law, not just the moral law. Every precept of the *tôrâ* must be observed; one may not pick and choose.

Now we must recognize that there is a certain truth to the claim that the law exhibits a unity and stands as a unit. It is also true that the Bible does not classify laws according to a scheme such as moral, civil and ceremonial. But that argument holds true for most of theology as well. Nowhere does the Bible summarize most of our schemes found in systematic theology. The word "trinity," for example, is never found as such, but that does not mean that it is an improper conclusion. The only question should be: Is this categorization fair to the Biblical text? On that point there is a large body of teaching.

First of all, the ceremonial legislation had a built-in warning that it would only remain in effect until the real, to which it pointed, came. This built-in obsolescence was signaled in the text from the moment that the legislation on the tabernacle and its services was first given. It is contained in the word "pattern" found in Exod 25:8, 40. This meant that the tabernacle, its priests, its sacrifices, and its associated ritual looked forward to the redemptive work of the Savior. In the meantime men and women had to be satisfied with that which was only a copy, a pattern, a shadow, a type of the real, the actual, the antitype that was to come. When that came all models, copies and patterns would be instantaneously rendered obsolete. It is no wonder then that our Lord set forth in a number of the prophetic texts a deliberate priority and ranking of the legal injunctions that had been given by Moses. For instance, Hosea depicted God as saying, "For I desire mercy, not sacrifice" (Hos 6:6a). Similar sentiments are expressed in Isa 1: 11-17; Jer 7:21-23; Mic 6:8; 1 Sam 15:22-23; Ps 51:16-17. Therefore the notion that there is some type of division within the law is not a concept that has been imposed on it from the outside. The ceremonial laws were designed from their initiation to go out of vogue when the redemptive purpose for which they were given was reached, but that in no way prejudices the case for the other aspects of the law of Moses that did not have this same warning about their pending obsolescence as did the parts relating to the tabernacle and its services in Exodus 25 through Leviticus 17. A fair interpretation of the Bible demands that we recognize a fundamental difference between those aspects of the law that reflect God's character and those that symbolically point to the first and second coming of Christ and command only a temporary hold over believers with a stated expiration period.

This argument that the *tôrâ* is a unity can also be used against the position that seeks totally to disengage the gospel from any relationship to the law. That same law of Moses in Genesis to Deuteronomy includes the promise and the Abrahamic covenant as well as the legal aspects. Therefore if Paul's *nomos* is not just an aspect of the "law" he refutes, then Paul abolishes the promise aspects of *tôrâ* as well. We cannot have it both ways.

Do the penalties of the law continue to be an integral part of that law?

It is impossible, we are told by strict law-gospel separationists as well as by dominion-theology advocates, to have the law of God without accepting all of its sanctions and penalties as well. The law cannot be divorced from its proper penalties; otherwise it merely becomes good advice. As surely as law embodies the essential ideas of command and obligation, it must likewise embody the idea of sanction.

Two different agendas are at work on the modern scene. One wants to prevent believers from emptying the cross of Christ of the fact that our Lord paid for the curse of the law that was set against all of us. Although that point is well taken, to argue from it to the position that since our Lord took care of the legal sanctions that were set against us we are no longer bound by anything in the law falls into the opposite ditch of demeaning the revelation of the Word and, ultimately, the character of God. Indeed the law does have a "ministry of death" and "of condemnation" (2 Cor 3:7, 9), it does "work wrath" (Rom 4:15), and "as many as are of the works of the law are under the curse" (Gal 3:10). All of this is to presume, however, that these texts have spoken comprehensively and definitively on all aspects and purposes of the law. But just as the knowledge of Christ reflected through the believer is "to the one . . . the smell of death . . . and to the other the fragrance of life" (2 Cor 2:16), so the law of God will produce different effects upon people, depending on their heart's preparation for it.

Moreover the same OT law could be enjoined upon a NT believer without carrying over the same punishment prescribed in the OT. Although the law's proscription against incest and sexual immorality was relevant for the Corinthian church (1 Cor 5:1-5), Paul did not recommend the death penalty found in Lev 20:11 (cf. 18:8; Deut 22: 30; 27:20) but that the individual be given church discipline until he repented and was restored. The same law of God was still in effect without demanding that the same sanction be attached. Thus the law remained applicable even though the sanction was changed.

The second agenda is found in reconstructionism or dominion theology. Bahnsen, for example, comes to the conclusion that since "God's law is binding in every detail until and unless the Lawgiver reveals otherwise, . . . the civil magistrate today ought to apply the penal sanctions of the Old Testament law to criminals in our society."[4]

It is in this area of penal sanctions that the most notorious disagreements between Reformed theologians and reconstructionists break out. The sharpest criticism of the theonomist's position on sanctions has been leveled by Meredith G. Kline's "intrusionist" ethics.[5] Kline argues that much of Israel's social and political law functions now to prefigure the holiness of God's kingdom and thereby belongs to the consummation of all things. Therefore the Mosaic law as a system is no longer binding on us. The typology that it prefigured has been fulfilled in Christ.

Kline's intrusionism does not appear to differ much from distinctive dispensationalist approaches to the law. Both positions would affirm the termination of the law and the presence of types in the OT. Their only difference would be in deciding on individual values for the types and what constituted legitimate antitypes. We are still left without an explanation as to how these legal texts function for the contemporary Christian. Especially in the wake of *Roe v. Wade* and the abortion fiasco that has come upon America since 1973, an answer that these texts had a different meaning in the pre-Christian era than they do today is not acceptable. Furthermore the details of the text usually are swallowed up in a widesweeping generalization about the history of salvation being fulfilled in Christ.

The key text in this discussion is Num 35:31: "Do not accept a ransom [or substitute] for the life of a murderer, who deserves to die. He must surely be put to death." There were some sixteen crimes that called for the death penalty in the OT: premeditated murder, kidnapping, adultery, homosexuality, incest, bestiality, incorrigible delinquency in a child, striking or cursing parents, offering a human sacrifice, false prophecy, blasphemy, profaning the Sabbath, sacrificing to false gods, magic and divination, unchastity, rape of a betrothed virgin. Only in the case of premeditated murder did the text say that the officials in Israel were forbidden to take a "ransom" or a "substitute." This has been widely interpreted to imply that in all the other fifteen cases the judges could commute the crimes deserving of capital punishment by designating a "ransom" or "substitute." In that case the death penalty served to mark the seriousness of the crime. Note that only God could say which crimes might have their sanctions ransomed.[6]

Bahnsen rejects such an explanation, complaining that "at best it appeals to a fallacious argument from silence" and "it fails to show that the penal sanctions have been laid aside *in general*."[7] But as Bahnsen acknowledges, he must on the other hand presume the continuing validity of these sanctions and wonder why Paul did not make any reference to them, especially when he had direct occasion to do so because of his handling exactly the same type of cases - for example, incest - in 1Corinthians 5.[8] This is not to argue that we believe that the OT penal sanctions were too severe, barbaric or crude, as if they failed to match a much more urbane and cultured day such as ours is. Bahnsen appropriately notes that in Heb 2:2 "every violation and disobedience received its just [or appropriate] punishment"[9] – that is, the God who prescribes the penalty can also say under what conditions it may be handled by a substitute. We conclude that not all the sanctions of OT law continue to our day. In fact, some were already being commuted in the OT.

Did the law ever offer, even hypothetically, eternal life to any who obeyed?

"Hypothetically," writes Alva J. McClain, "the law could give life if men kept it."[10] The alleged proof for this bold claim is usually Lev 18: 5: "Keep my decrees and laws, for the man who obeys them will live by them. I am the Lord." The same sentiment, it is further alleged, is found three times in Ezek 20:11, 13, 21: "For the man who obeys them will live by them." Our Lord is said to have offered the same plan to the rich young ruler in Matt 19:17: "If you want to enter life, obey the commandments." Finally, the apostle Paul described the righteousness that is in the law in Rom 10:5: "The man who does these things will live by them." Again in Gal 3:12 Paul contrasts the righteousness based on faith with "the man who does these things [living] . . . by them."

It would appear at first reading of these texts that the law certainly offered some type of life if a person could perfectly keep it. But this conclusion cannot be sustained by a fair treatment of these texts in their context or with parallel texts from both Testaments. I would urge the

Church to drop all statements that teach or imply that there is another way of salvation offered in the Bible – even if only hypothetically.

The so-called legalistic "if" of Exod 19:8; 24:3, 7 is no more conditional for salvation than the same conditions and commands given to Abraham ("Leave your country," Gen 12:1; "Walk before me and be blameless," 17:1; "Keep the way of the Lord by doing what is right and just," 18:19) or to the contemporary believer in Jesus Christ ("If you love me, you will obey what I command," John 14:15; "If you obey my commands, you will remain in my love," 15:10; "If you want to enter life, obey the commandments," Matt 19:17). Hence the same unconditional covenant with Abraham continues with the same promises into the Mosaic law of the Sinaitic covenant.

The conditionality found in most of these passages does not relate to salvation in either the OT or the NT. It has to do with the quality of life lived in the promise and the joy of participating in all the benefits of that promise.[11]

Andrew A. Bonar is representative of those who in another generation missed the proper interpretation of Lev 18:5:

> But if, as most think, we are to take in this place the words, "*live in them*" as meaning "eternal life to be got by them," the scope of the passage is that so excellent are God's laws, and every special minute detail of these laws, *that if a man were to keep these always and perfectly*, this keeping would be eternal life to him. And the quotations in Rom. x. 5, and Gal. iii. 12, would seem to determine this to be the true and only sense here.[12]

This view misses these crucial points: (1) "These things" in Lev 18:5 are the statutes of the Lord placed in contrast with the customs and practices of the Canaanites and Egyptians; (2) the passage in Leviticus 18 is framed with the theological setting of the first and last verses addressed to those who know that "I am the Lord your God";

(3) one of the ways of "doing" the law was to recognize that that same law made provision for those who failed to keep the law in that it provided for sacrifices and forgiveness of one's sins.

A much safer guide for understanding such texts is Patrick Fairbairn:

> Neither Moses nor Ezekiel, it is obvious, meant that the life spoken of, which comprehends whatever is really excellent and good, was to be *acquired* by means of such conformity to the enactments of heaven; for life in that sense already was theirs. . . . Doing these things, they lived in them; because life thus had its due exercise and nourishment and was in a condition to enjoy the manifold privileges and blessings secured in the covenant. And the very same may be said of the precepts and ordinances of the gospel: a man lives after the higher life of faith only insofar as he walks in conformity with these; for though he gets life by a simple act of faith in Christ, he cannot exercise, maintain and enjoy it but in connection with the institutions and requirements of the gospel.[13]

Indeed the gospel itself had been proclaimed to those individuals who died in the wilderness (Heb 4:2). So salvation has always been by grace and never by works, lest any man or woman should ever boast. There never was an alternate route to eternal life offered in the OT.

Was the law in general, and the decalogue in particular, addressed to Israel and not to all mankind?

"It was to Israel that the Decalogue was primarily addressed, and not to all mankind," argued John R. Sampey.[14] The law viewed as a law code, it is frequently alleged, was given to Israel but was not meant for Gentiles or for times beyond those mentioned in the original setting in which it was given. Thus the Israelite would be "under" this Mosaic code until he could find the freedom and forgiveness that would later be offered under grace in Christ through the new covenant.

If this claim of Israelite exclusivity is true, however, why did the Gentiles who did not have the law of God have that law written on their hearts? That was Paul's testimony in Rom 2:12-16. It would appear that all peoples were under obligation to the same standard set forth in the law of God.

In fact Lev 24:22 advocated: "You are to have the same law for the alien and the native-born. I am the Lord your God." Scripture rejected any type of double standard of morality. Accordingly the prophetic standard lifted up the same single standard of the law of God: "All the nations will stream to [Jerusalem in that day]. . . . [They] will come and say, 'Come, let us go up to the mountain of the Lord, to the house of the God of Jacob. He will teach us his ways, so that we may walk in his paths.' The law will go out of Zion, the word of the Lord from Jerusalem" (Isa 2:2-3). Added to this argument is the fact that Solomon's Proverbs were addressed universally to all, but what many fail to realize is that the Proverbs are in the main nothing more than a popularization of the precepts found in the Mosaic law.

The fact that God judged the nations of antiquity (as he still does today) by the same standard of righteousness that he expected of Israel is clear from the numerous warnings given to Israel as they were entering the land of Canaan. For example, Lev 18:26-28 warns: "But you must keep my decrees and my laws. . . . And if you defile the land [by disobeying these laws], it will vomit you out as it vomited out the nations that were before you." And Deut 2:10-23 teaches that even the nations that occupied Canaan prior to Israel's conquest had been given those very same lands because of the defilements of God's law by the previous occupants. Thus a prophet like Amos read the riot act to each of the six nations surrounding eighth-century Israel and Judah because they, without actual copies of the law of God, nevertheless also offended God's high moral standard and were thereby judged by the same law. In fact what one pagan king did to another pagan king in violation of the concept of the image of God stirred the just ire of God and the condemnation of the prophet Amos (Amos 2:1-3).

Thus far we are in agreement with Bahnsen and the reconstructionists. Would that more of God's people caught the same vision that bravely declares that when any modern nation sins against the law of God that nation is in serious trouble with the Sovereign of the universe! If God judged the Third Reich of Germany in part because Hitler gassed six million Jews with little or no protest from the people of God in that land, what will God do to the United States for deliberately aborting twenty-two million babies in less than twenty years? The fact that *Roe v. Wade* caught the Church off guard in 1973 with no teaching is precisely related to our failure to teach the whole counsel of God, including the law of God, to the Church. The Church may yet pay dearly for this neglect.

But what about the OT's teaching on civil magistrates? May we proceed from the descriptive passages of the OT to anything more than principial guidelines for government? Or must we, as Bahnsen assumes, adopt in detail the model of government under the theocracy as the basis for all righteous government today?

We have no problem with the principles laid down for governments in general in Deuteronomy or Proverbs or as illustrated in the prophetic messages. But we cannot argue as Bahnsen does that "Israel's law was a *model* for all the nations round about. And it was such a model with respect to *all* the statutes delivered from God through Moses – including, then, the statutes touching on political matters like crime and punishment."[15]

Bahnsen does yield the argument to the extent that he admits that "not everything about ancient Israel is to be made part of our modern political experience. . . . We are concerned simply with the *standing laws of civil justice*. 'Holy War' during Israel's conquering of the promised land was by God's direct and specific command, for a set time and place. . . ; it was not standing civil policy for all men (any more than the specific command for Samuel to anoint David king of Israel at a set time and place)."[16] What then are "standing laws" for Bahnsen?

> "Standing law" is used here for *policy* directives applicable over time to classes of individuals (e.g., do not kill; children, obey your parents; merchants, have equal measures; magistrates, execute rapists), in contrast to particular directions for an individual (e.g., the order for Samuel to

anoint David at a particular time and place) or positive commands for distinct incidents (e.g., God's order for Israel to exterminate certain Canaanite tribes at a certain point in history).[17]

Surely this classification has brought us a long way to moving together. Positive law and individual directives ought not to be included in those principles that have abiding force even if those particularistic commands probably illustrate a universal principle behind them much as the apostle Paul's injunction that Euodia and Syntyche "agree with each other in the Lord" (Phil 4:2) illustrates the command to "be kind and compassionate to one another, forgiving each other" (Eph 4:32).

What is needed for rapprochement now is to check each other's list of "standing laws" for hermeneutical consistency. The key question will revolve around the Covenant Code and those laws that belong to that same general category. In my view, the laws of Exodus 21-23 are illustrations of the Ten Commandments. In fact I have argued that the various specifications of Deuteronomy 12-25 follow the exact order and illustrate the principles laid down in the Decalogue.[18] To continue to insist that Christians should not muzzle oxen, for example, misses the abiding truth and fails to acknowledge that we are dealing with a particular genre of case law.

While it is true that the law is given for all nations, times and peoples, I cannot agree that each of the capital punishments is still in vogue – except for murder, which has as its reason a moral principle: People are made in the image of God. Nor should we attempt to replicate in detail all the laws given for judges and magistrates in Exodus 21-23 and repeated to some extent in Deuteronomy. This would be a hermeneutical failure to observe that we are here dealing with case law that is based on applying precedents. Therefore we too must search for those same precedents contained in these laws and use them to guide our society without imposing or prescribing the exact details of previous cases. Our method for applying such a "ladder of abstraction" I have traced out elsewhere.[19]

Is the law of the new covenant the same law meant for the church?

A new setting for the stalemate over law and grace is now possible as a result of the dramatic change effected around 1965. It was about that time that dispensationalists decided that no longer would they hold to two new covenants,[20] one for the Church and one for Israel. Even though Jer 31:31 clearly affirmed that God had directed the "new covenant" to "the house of Israel and . . . the house of Judah," it was now seen that the Church was also involved.[21]

The identical point has also been raised recently by Bruce Waltke. While commenting on the phenomenon of conditionality within the unconditional covenants, he affirms that "Jeremiah unmistakably shows [the new covenant's] continuity with the provisions of the old law."[22] With respect to the promise of God in the new covenant that he would "put [his] law in their minds" (Jer 31:33), Waltke correctly asserts that "the 'law' in view here is unquestionably the Mosaic treaty. It is summarized by the expression 'Know YHWH.' . . . In short, the new covenant assumes the content of the old Mosaic treaty. But its [new] form is like that of YHWH's grants to Abraham and David.

Unlike the Mosaic treaty that rested on Israel's willingness to keep it, YHWH will unilaterally put his law in Israel's heart."[23]

It is now possible for us to see why it is not fair for contemporary scholars to continue affirming that "as long as the covenant with Moses was in effect Israel was obligated to keep the entire law. (Division of the Mosaic law into distinct categories – such as civil, ceremonial, and moral – was unknown to the OT Israelite. Within the theocracy the law of Moses was a unified entity.)"[24] Once the Mosaic law is seen as a legitimate part of the substance of the new covenant the whole dispute has suddenly been put on another plane. Evangelical theology must now undergo the same painful process of retraction that many had to undergo when it suddenly became evident that there was only one new covenant and not two. It is precisely this phenomenon of conditionality within all of the unconditional covenants that alerted us to the fact that God's grace is not disturbed by the repeated failure of some or even all of those to whom grace is extended.

In fact, evangelicals should have been alerted to the fact that God's moral law was already part of his promise plan when he said of Abraham in Gen 26:5 that "Abraham obeyed my voice (*šāmaʿ běqōlî*) and kept my charge (*wayyišmōr mišmartî*), my commandments (*miṣwôtay*), my statutes (*huqqôtay*) and my laws (*tôrōtay*)." So startling was this verse in its implications that even the conservative Delitzsch exclaimed: "Undoubtedly verse 5 in this passage is from the hand of the Deuteronomist."[25] The point is that these were the very terms that would be used later on to describe the Mosaic law. But that is the point I wish to make: So endemic is the moral law to the whole of the Mosaic law that evidences for its abiding nature can be found in the fact that even before it was given on Sinai it was held to be normative and binding on all who aspired to living by faith. In fact every one of the Ten Commandments is already implicitly found in the Genesis record even before their publication on Sinai.[26] Moses did not invent the moral law; God did, and he had already been holding men and women responsible for heeding it millennia before he finally wrote it on tablets of stone.

Questions we must ask about Gen 26:5 are these: How could Abraham have obeyed the Mosaic law when it had not in fact been given as yet to Moses? Why is Abraham credited with keeping the law when the patriarchal narrative takes such great pains to let us know that Abraham, Isaac and Jacob lived by faith? Why does the text so suddenly mention anyone keeping God's charge, his commandments, his statutes, and his laws, when nothing has been stated or even implied in the text to prepare us for such a novel idea?[27]

It is doubtful that the later Mosaic law is being retrojected back onto the Abrahamic situation in an attempt to read the parts of the Pentateuch in light of the whole. Such a thesis would allow the interests of an alleged redactor to take precedence over that of revelation from God, the latter being a claim that the text makes for itself. Instead this is another case of what Paul alluded to when he claimed in Romans that those who do not have the moral law of God written as it appeared in the Mosaic code demonstrate that that law nevertheless has been impressed upon their consciences and in their hearts. That is why they either accuse or excuse themselves on many of these same issues, all the while remaining without the actual written text itself. If that is still true of the pagan outside of Christ today, why could it not also be true of everyone prior to the revelation of the law to Moses?

Conclusion

It should be evident by now that the law can and must be viewed as being divided into various components with the moral aspect of that one law of God being the most basic, enduring and normative of the various parts. The fact that the patriarchs were already living in accordance with such a law prior to Sinai, yet without jeopardizing the reality of God's grace, his promise of the gospel, or thereby advocating an alleged works-salvation, should go a long way toward demonstrating that these two elements of faith and obedience are not necessarily antithetical offers in the plan of God. Add to this the clear statement of our Lord in Matt 23:23 ff., teaching that indeed some things in the law carried more weight than its other aspects, and the case is closed. No wonder the prophets placed a higher priority on the moral aspects of the law over its ceremonial obligations!

For the same reasons I likewise find defective the idea that the penalties of the law are as much an integral part of the law even for our day as are its moral parts. Nor did that law ever offer salvation to anyone who could perfectly maintain it, even on a hypothetical basis. In both of these cases the exegetical grounds for these arguments are flawed, as I have argued above.

Rather, the moral law of God is the foundational aspect of the whole law, and its address is to all persons in all times, including our own. To so emphasize grace to the exclusion of resulting obligation to the moral law of God will land our present-day churches precisely where they find themselves in the current cultural morass. Several recent surveys of the moral and ethical attitudes of our younger evangelical constituencies go a long way toward establishing that many of these believers act and think about many ethical issues almost exactly as do their unbelieving counterparts in the contemporary culture. This only points to a hiatus in the teaching program of the Church.

One evidence of the tremendous gulf that exists between belief and ethical action can be seen in the overwhelming response found in evangelical circles for seminars that take the book of Proverbs as a set of answers to some of society's basic conflicts. But what does Proverbs state in short, epigrammatic form that was not first stated in the moral law of God in the Pentateuch? Even a casual perusal of the marginal references in some recent editions of the book of Proverbs will demonstrate that these proverbs and the great body of wisdom literature in the OT are deeply indebted to Exodus, Numbers and Deuteronomy where the moral law of God is either set forth or illustrated.

I conclude that too much confidence has been placed in the hermeneutical judgment that the law is so unified that when Christ fulfilled its ceremonial aspects the whole law ended its claim over today's believers. Such an all-or-nothing argument has resulted in the premature confidence that the law has nothing to say to the believer. Is it any wonder then that the Church was caught off guard by the abortion issue in 1973? Of course the NT nowhere takes up the topic of abortion. Consequently, contemporary believers ask, if we are living under grace, can we not each exercise our own freedom as we see fit? God forbid! And what will we say about euthanasia, bestiality, marrying one's own family members, *in vitro* fertilization and a hundred other topics that our complex age waits to ask of those who claim to have a revelation from God? This discussion is no longer a spiritual luxury; it involves the real lives of real people.

I would urge believers to flee first of all to the grace of God found in his gracious promise of salvation. But I would also urge that they move just as decisively in demonstrating the reality of that gracious gift of God by the way the moral law of God is heeded in every area of life. Just as Abraham believed and then obeyed, so we too must live.

If the same *tôrâ* that God gave to Moses was made part of the new covenant, then it should be abundantly clear that our Lord still wants that law, at least in its weightier parts, to exercise a control over how we ought to act and live. The conditional aspects of the law no more handicap grace or truncate its blessings than they impugned the unilateral aspects of the Abrahamic or Davidic covenants, which likewise had "if" clauses and commands attached to their covenants that clearly depended solely and totally on God's commitment to fulfill his promise. Biblical law and the gospel of God's grace are not archrivals but twin mercies given by the same gracious Lord who did not wish his people in any age to be impoverished but to enjoy life to the fullest.

Footnotes

1. G. L. Bahnsen, *Theonomy in Christian Ethics* (Phillipsburg: Craig, 1977). In an attempt to set forth a summary of *Theonomy* as well as set the stage for a new book, *Debate Over God's Law*, Bahnsen wrote *By This Standard: The Authority of God's Law Today* (Tyler: Institute for Christian Economics, 1985).

2. The foundation for Bahnsen's work may be found in R. J. Rushdoony, *The Institutes of Biblical Law* (Phillipsburg: Craig, 1973). In addition to Rushdoony's work the following have also played a part in dominion theology: G. North, *The Dominion Covenant: Genesis* (Tyler: Institute for Christian Economics, 1982); *Moses and Pharaoh: Dominion Religion Versus Power Religion* (Tyler: Institute for Christian Economics, 1984); *Backward, Christian Soldiers? An Action Manual for Christian Reconstruction* (Tyler: Institute for Christian Economics, 1985); *An Introduction to Christian Economics* (Phillipsburg: Craig, 1973); D. Chilton, *Paradise Restored: A Biblical Theology of Dominion* (Tyler: Institute for Christian Economics, 1985); *Productive Christians in an Age of Guilt-Manipulators* (Tyler: Institute for Christian Economics, 1985); J. B. Jordan, *The Law of the Covenant: An Exposition of Exodus 21-23* (Tyler: Institute for Christian Economics, 1984).

3. H. A. W. Meyer writes: "In *nomos*, however, to think merely of the moral law is erroneous; and the distinction between the ritualistic, civil, and moral law is modern" ("Matthew," in *Commentary on the New Testament* [New York: Funk and Wagnalls, 1884]), 1. 120. Similarly A. S. Peake, "Colossians," in *The Expositor's Greek Testament* (Grand Rapids: Eerdmans, 1967), 3.527, says, "But this distinction between the moral and ceremonial Law has no meaning

in Paul. The Law is a unity and is done away as a whole"; cf. similarly A. J. McClain, *Law and Grace* (Chicago: Moody, 1954) 10-12. D. J. Moo, "'Law,' 'Works of the Law,' and Legalism in Paul," *WTJ* 45 (1983) 84, affirms that *"nomos* is basically for Paul a single indivisible whole. . . . Paul's argument prohibits a neat distinction of moral and ceremonial law." A year later, however, Moo wrote: "While it is true that a theoretical distinction [between the moral and ceremonial law]... was not made, there emerges, for instance in Philo and at Qumran, a *practical* differentiation of this nature. Jesus' appropriation of the prophetic emphasis on the need for *inner* obedience, his comment about 'the weightier matters', the elevation of the love command. . . all suggest that he may have operated with a similar distinction. . . . It is not illegitimate to find the seeds of this kind of distinction in passages such as Mark 7:1-23" ("Jesus and the Authority of the Mosaic Law," *JSNT* 20 [1984] 15 [italics his]).

4   Bahnsen, *By This Standard* 270-271. Bahnsen emphasized the first half of this citation with italics.

5   M. G. Kline, "Comments on an Old-New Error," *WTJ* 41 (1978-79) 172-189. Bahnsen's reply is found in "M. G. Kline on Theonomic Politics: An Evaluation of His Reply," *The Journal of Christian Reconstruction* 6 (1979-80) 195-221.

6   W. C. Kaiser, Jr., *Toward Old Testament Ethics* (Grand Rapids: Zondervan, 1983) 91-92.

7   Bahnsen, *By This Standard* 282.

8   Ibid. 283.

9   Ibid. 279.

10 A. J. McClain, *Law and Grace* 17. *The Scofield Reference Bible* (1945) 20 n. 1 contends that Israel spoke "rashly" when they pledged in Exod 19:8; 24:3, 7: "We will do everything the Lord has said." Scofield taught that Israel moved from "believing" now to "doing" as the basis for her spiritual life. Cf., however, the Lord's assessment: "Oh, that their hearts would be inclined to fear me and to keep my commands always, so that it might go well with them and their children forever!" (Deut 5:28-29).

11 See a fuller explanation of these matters in W. C. Kaiser, Jr., "Leviticus 18:5 and Paul: 'Do This and You Shall Live' (Eternally?)," *JETS* 14 (1971) 19-28.

12 A. A. Bonar, *A Commentary on Leviticus* (London: Banner of Truth, 1966 [1846] 329-330 [italics his]). C. L. Feinberg, *The Prophecy of Ezekiel* (Chicago: Moody, 1969) 110, similarly says, "Obedience would have brought life physically and spiritually, temporally and eternally."

13 P. Fairbairn, *An Exposition of Ezekiel* (Evansville: Sovereign Grace, 1960) 215-216 (italics his).

[14] J. R. Sampey, "The Ten Commandments," in *International Standard Bible Encyclopedia* (Grand Rapids: Eerdmans, 1952), 5.2944.

[15] Bahnsen, *By This Standard* 237.

[16] Ibid. 322-323 (italics his).

[17] Ibid. 346 n. 1 (italics his).

[18] Kaiser, Ethics 127-137.

[19] W. C. Kaiser, Jr., *Toward Rediscovering the Old Testament* (Grand Rapids: Zondervan, 1987) 155-166 (note the diagram on p. 166); cf. also "A Case for a Single Ethic in Business," in *Foundational Questions to a Biblical View of Business* (ed. R.C. Chewning; Colorado Springs: NavPress, 1989) 76-88.

[20] J. D. Pentecost, *Things to Come: A Study of Biblical Eschatology* (Grand Rapids: Zondervan, 1971) 121-128, discusses three views on the relationship of the new covenant to the Church: J. N. Darby's view of one and only one new covenant that has no relationship to the Church, C. I. Scofield's view that there is one new covenant with a present application to the Church now and a future application to national Israel, and L. S. Chafer's view that there are two new covenants (one with Israel as promised in Jer 31:31-34 and one made with the Church in this present age). J. F. Walvoord, "The New Covenant with Israel," *BSac* 110 (1953) 204, says, "The concept of two new covenants is a better analysis of the problem." All of this has quietly been changing since 1965 in most dispensationalist presentations. For example R. L. Saucy, *The Church in God's Program* (Chicago: Moody, 1972) 78, boldly asserts: "The Scriptures, however, do not reveal a separate new covenant [for the church]." On p. 80 he continues: "Although the Old Testament references to the new covenant were for the nation of Israel, the members of the church also share in its provisions."

[21] See W. C. Kaiser, Jr., "The Old Promise and the New Covenant: Jeremiah 31:31-34," *JETS* 15 (1972) 11-23, reprinted in *The Bible and Its Literary Milieu: Contemporary Essays* (ed. V. L. Toilers and J. R. Maier; Grand Rapids: Eerdmans, 1979) 106-120.

[22] B. K. Waltke, "The Phenomenon of Conditionality Within the Unconditional Covenants," in *Israel's Apostasy and Restoration: Essays in Honor of Roland K. Harrison* (ed. A. Gileadi; Grand Rapids: Baker, 1988) 136-137.

[23] Ibid.

[24] M. W. Karlberg, "The Significance of Israel in Biblical Typology," *JETS* 31 (1988) 263. Karlberg also quotes F. F. Bruce to the same effect: "If we like, we may say that Paul has the moral law mainly in mind [in Gal 3:24-25], whereas the author of Hebrews is concerned more with the ceremonial law – although the distinction between the moral and ceremonial law is drawn by Christian

theologians, not by those who accepted the whole law as the will of God, nor yet by the New Testament writers" (*The Epistle to the Hebrews* [NICNT; Grand Rapids: Eerdmans, 1964] 145). Likewise D. A. Carson observes that "it is common to distinguish between moral, ceremonial and civil law. . . . The distinction. . . is apt, especially in terms of functional description, but it is not self-evident that either Old Testament or New Testament writers neatly classify Old Testament law in those categories in such a way as to establish continuity and discontinuity on the basis of such distinctions" ("Jesus and the Sabbath in the Four Gospels," in *From Sabbath to Lord's Day: A Biblical, Historical, and Theological Investigation* [ed. D. A. Carson; Grand Rapids: Zondervan, 1982] 74). On p. 91 n. 74 Carson qualifies his disclaimer by saying, "This is not to deny that 'moral law' exists, in the sense of unchangeable prescriptions of right and wrong, or that some laws are ceremonial and others are civil. But I question the view that this classic three-fold distinction was used by New Testament writers in their presentation of the relationship between law and gospel." Given what I have argued above – namely, that Jesus appealed to just such a distinction – and given the reappearance of the Mosaic law in the new covenant, the recognition of the presence of these three forms of the law may be just what is needed in our circles once again.

[25] F. Delitzsch, *A New Commentary on Genesis* (Edinburgh: T. and T. Clark, 1888) 137 ff. Likewise the conservative C. F. Keil recognized that these were the terms later to be used to describe the Mosaic law (*Biblical Commentary on the Old Testament* [Grand Rapids: Eerdmans, 1971] 270).

[26] The evidence for the presence of all Ten Commandments being found in Genesis is found in Kaiser, *Ethics* 81-82.

[27] I have been aided in formulating these questions by reading an unpublished manuscript of my colleague John Sailhamer. The point I am making, however, is altogether different from the one he makes of these same questions. He is not responsible for my usage here.